EMMANUEL JOSEPH

Humanitarian Soldiers, When Aid Meets Military in the UK

Copyright © 2025 by Emmanuel Joseph

All rights reserved. No part of this publication may be reproduced, stored or transmitted in any form or by any means, electronic, mechanical, photocopying, recording, scanning, or otherwise without written permission from the publisher. It is illegal to copy this book, post it to a website, or distribute it by any other means without permission.

First edition

This book was professionally typeset on Reedsy.
Find out more at reedsy.com

Contents

1. Chapter 1: The Convergence of Humanitarianism and Military — 1
2. Chapter 2: Historical Context and Evolution — 3
3. Chapter 3: Training Humanitarian Soldiers — 5
4. Chapter 4: Humanitarian Soldiers in Action — 7
5. Chapter 5: Challenges and Ethical Dilemmas — 9
6. Chapter 6: Case Studies from the UK — 11
7. Chapter 7: The Role of Technology — 13
8. Chapter 8: Collaboration with Humanitarian Organizations — 15
9. Chapter 9: Gender and Diversity in Humanitarian Military... — 17
10. Chapter 10: The Future of Humanitarian Military Cooperation — 19
11. Chapter 11: Lessons Learned and Best Practices — 21
12. Chapter 12: A Vision for the Future — 23

1

Chapter 1: The Convergence of Humanitarianism and Military

Humanitarian aid and military operations have long been seen as disparate entities with contrasting principles. Humanitarianism emphasizes neutrality, impartiality, and the alleviation of human suffering. In contrast, military operations focus on achieving strategic objectives, often involving force. However, the evolving nature of global conflicts and disasters has necessitated a convergence of these fields. In the UK, this interplay has led to innovative strategies that combine the strengths of both sectors. Humanitarian soldiers emerge as agents of change, navigating the complex landscape where aid meets military intervention.

In recent years, the UK's military has increasingly engaged in humanitarian missions. This shift reflects a broader recognition that addressing the root causes of conflict and instability requires a multifaceted approach. Humanitarian soldiers are trained not only in combat but also in disaster response, medical assistance, and community engagement. This dual capacity enables them to provide immediate relief while also working towards long-term stability. The integration of humanitarian principles into military training represents a significant evolution in the role of the armed forces.

One of the key challenges in this convergence is maintaining the principles of neutrality and impartiality. Humanitarian soldiers must navigate the delicate balance between military objectives and the imperative to provide unbiased aid. This requires a deep understanding of the local context, cultural sensitivity, and the ability to build trust with affected communities. The UK's experience in various conflict zones has highlighted the importance of these skills. Humanitarian soldiers often act as mediators, bridging the gap between military forces and civilians.

The collaboration between humanitarian organizations and the military has also led to the development of new frameworks and protocols. These guidelines ensure that humanitarian principles are upheld while leveraging the logistical capabilities of the military. In the UK, initiatives such as the Civil-Military Cooperation Centre of Excellence have been instrumental in fostering this cooperation. By sharing knowledge and resources, humanitarian soldiers can enhance the effectiveness of aid delivery and contribute to more sustainable outcomes.

In summary, the convergence of humanitarianism and military operations in the UK represents a paradigm shift in the approach to global crises. Humanitarian soldiers embody the synthesis of these fields, bringing together the strengths of both sectors to address complex challenges. Their role requires a unique set of skills, including cultural sensitivity, strategic thinking, and a commitment to humanitarian principles. As the nature of conflicts and disasters continues to evolve, the importance of humanitarian soldiers will only grow.

2

Chapter 2: Historical Context and Evolution

The relationship between humanitarian aid and military intervention has a long and complex history. In the UK, this relationship has evolved significantly over the past century. Early examples of military involvement in humanitarian efforts can be traced back to the aftermath of World War I. The establishment of the League of Nations and subsequent humanitarian missions marked the beginning of a new era in which military forces played a role in addressing humanitarian crises. This period laid the foundation for the modern concept of humanitarian soldiers.

During World War II, the UK military's involvement in humanitarian efforts expanded significantly. The war's widespread devastation created an urgent need for coordinated relief efforts. The military played a crucial role in delivering aid to affected populations, both within the UK and abroad. This period also saw the emergence of international organizations such as the United Nations, which formalized the principles of humanitarianism. The experiences of World War II highlighted the importance of cooperation between military and humanitarian actors.

The post-war period brought new challenges and opportunities for humanitarian soldiers. The Cold War era was characterized by proxy conflicts and regional crises, many of which required humanitarian intervention. The UK's military was often called upon to provide assistance in conflict zones, from the Korean War to the Falklands conflict. These missions underscored the need for specialized training in humanitarian principles and the importance of maintaining neutrality in politically charged environments. The concept of humanitarian soldiers continued to evolve, reflecting the changing nature of global conflicts.

In the 1990s, the UK military's role in humanitarian efforts expanded further with the advent of peacekeeping missions. The conflicts in the Balkans, Rwanda, and Sierra Leone highlighted the need for a comprehensive approach to humanitarian intervention. Humanitarian soldiers were tasked with providing protection to civilians, delivering aid, and supporting post-conflict reconstruction. These missions required a deep understanding of the local context and the ability to work closely with humanitarian organizations. The experiences of this period shaped the modern framework for humanitarian military engagement.

Today, the UK's military continues to play a vital role in humanitarian efforts around the world. The principles of neutrality and impartiality remain central to these missions, guiding the actions of humanitarian soldiers. The evolution of this role reflects a growing recognition of the interconnected nature of global crises. By combining the strengths of humanitarianism and military intervention, the UK has developed a unique approach to addressing complex challenges. The historical context provides valuable insights into the development of humanitarian soldiers and their ongoing importance.

3

Chapter 3: Training Humanitarian Soldiers

The transformation of military personnel into humanitarian soldiers requires a comprehensive and multifaceted training program. This program combines traditional military training with specialized education in humanitarian principles, cultural sensitivity, and disaster response. In the UK, this training is delivered through various institutions, including the Defence Academy and the Civil-Military Cooperation Centre of Excellence. The goal is to equip military personnel with the skills and knowledge needed to navigate the complex landscape of humanitarian operations.

One of the key components of this training is an understanding of international humanitarian law and the principles of neutrality, impartiality, and independence. Humanitarian soldiers must be able to apply these principles in diverse and challenging environments. This requires not only theoretical knowledge but also practical experience in simulated scenarios. Training exercises often involve collaboration with humanitarian organizations to ensure that military personnel are familiar with the operational realities of aid work.

Cultural sensitivity is another crucial aspect of training. Humanitarian soldiers must be able to engage with local communities in a respectful and empathetic manner. This involves learning about the history, traditions, and social dynamics of the regions in which they operate. Language skills are also important, as effective communication can help build trust and facilitate cooperation. The UK's diverse military force, with personnel from various cultural backgrounds, is well-positioned to develop these skills.

Medical training is also a key component of the program. Humanitarian soldiers are often called upon to provide medical assistance in disaster zones and conflict areas. This requires proficiency in first aid, trauma care, and disease prevention. In addition to physical health, soldiers are trained to address mental health issues, both among affected populations and within their own ranks. This holistic approach ensures that humanitarian soldiers can provide comprehensive care in a wide range of situations.

In summary, the training of humanitarian soldiers in the UK is a rigorous and multidisciplinary process. It prepares military personnel to operate effectively in complex and often volatile environments. By integrating humanitarian principles with military expertise, the UK has developed a cadre of soldiers who are uniquely equipped to address the challenges of modern humanitarian operations. This training not only enhances the capabilities of the armed forces but also contributes to more effective and ethical humanitarian interventions.

4

Chapter 4: Humanitarian Soldiers in Action

The deployment of humanitarian soldiers in the field showcases the practical application of their training and the unique contributions they make to humanitarian efforts. In recent years, the UK has deployed humanitarian soldiers to various conflict zones and disaster areas, demonstrating the effectiveness of this approach. Their work spans a range of activities, from providing medical assistance to rebuilding infrastructure and supporting local communities.

One notable example is the UK's involvement in the response to the Ebola outbreak in West Africa. Humanitarian soldiers played a crucial role in establishing treatment centers, providing medical care, and supporting efforts to contain the virus. Their military training enabled them to operate in challenging and high-risk environments, while their humanitarian training ensured that they adhered to principles of neutrality and impartiality. This mission highlighted the importance of a coordinated response that leverages both military and humanitarian capabilities.

In conflict zones, humanitarian soldiers often act as intermediaries between military forces and civilian populations. They work to build trust and facilitate communication, ensuring that aid reaches those in need while minimizing the risk of harm. In Syria, for example, UK humanitarian soldiers have been involved in delivering aid to besieged communities and supporting local relief efforts. Their presence helps to create a safer environment for humanitarian organizations to operate, bridging the gap between military objectives and humanitarian needs.

Disaster response is another area where humanitarian soldiers make a significant impact. In the aftermath of natural disasters, such as earthquakes and hurricanes, they provide immediate relief and support long-term recovery efforts. This includes search and rescue operations, medical assistance, and the reconstruction of critical infrastructure. In the Caribbean, UK humanitarian soldiers have been deployed to assist with disaster response and recovery, demonstrating the versatility and effectiveness of their training.

The experiences of humanitarian soldiers in the field also provide valuable insights for improving training and operational protocols. By documenting their experiences and sharing lessons learned, they contribute to the ongoing development of best practices in humanitarian military engagement. This iterative process ensures that the UK's approach to humanitarian intervention continues to evolve and adapt to changing global challenges.

In summary, humanitarian soldiers play a vital role in addressing complex humanitarian crises. Their unique training and capabilities enable them to operate effectively in diverse and challenging environments. By combining military expertise with a commitment to humanitarian principles, they provide essential support to affected populations and contribute to more effective and ethical humanitarian interventions. The deployment of humanitarian soldiers in the field underscores the importance of this innovative approach.

5

Chapter 5: Challenges and Ethical Dilemmas

The integration of humanitarian aid and military operations brings with it a host of challenges and ethical dilemmas. One of the primary challenges is maintaining the principles of neutrality and impartiality while carrying out military objectives. Humanitarian soldiers must navigate complex and often conflicting priorities, ensuring that their actions do not compromise the integrity of humanitarian assistance. This requires careful planning, coordination, and a deep commitment to ethical principles.

One ethical dilemma that arises is the potential for aid to be used as a tool of political or military strategy. In conflict zones, the distribution of aid can become entangled with broader geopolitical goals, leading to accusations of bias or manipulation. Humanitarian soldiers must be vigilant in ensuring that aid is distributed fairly and transparently, without favoritism or ulterior motives. This requires a clear separation of humanitarian and military roles, even as they work together towards common goals.

The presence of military forces in humanitarian operations can also pose risks to aid workers and beneficiaries. In some cases, the militarization of aid can lead to increased targeting of humanitarian personnel by armed groups. This underscores the importance of maintaining a distinct identity and operational approach for humanitarian soldiers. They must work to build trust with local communities and ensure that their actions are perceived as genuinely humanitarian rather than purely strategic.

Another challenge is the potential for mission creep, where military forces become increasingly involved in non-military tasks. While humanitarian soldiers are trained to provide immediate relief and support, their primary role remains that of a military force. Striking the right balance between humanitarian and military responsibilities is crucial to avoid overextension and ensure the effectiveness of both missions. Clear guidelines and protocols are essential to delineate the boundaries of their roles.

Finally, the psychological impact of humanitarian missions on military personnel is an important consideration. Humanitarian soldiers are often exposed to traumatic and emotionally challenging situations, from witnessing the suffering of civilians to dealing with the aftermath of natural disasters. Providing adequate mental health support and ensuring the well-being of humanitarian soldiers is critical to sustaining their effectiveness and resilience. This includes access to counseling, peer support, and resources for managing stress and trauma.

In summary, the convergence of humanitarian aid and military operations presents significant challenges and ethical dilemmas. Humanitarian soldiers must navigate these complexities with a strong commitment to ethical principles, transparency, and the well-being of both aid recipients and military personnel. By addressing these challenges thoughtfully and proactively, they can contribute to more effective and principled humanitarian interventions.

6

Chapter 6: Case Studies from the UK

To illustrate the practical application of humanitarian-military cooperation, it is helpful to examine specific case studies from the UK. These examples highlight the diverse ways in which humanitarian soldiers have contributed to addressing crises and supporting communities in need.

One notable case study is the UK's response to the 2015 Nepal earthquake. The British military played a pivotal role in delivering aid and providing medical assistance to affected communities. Humanitarian soldiers were deployed to remote areas to assess needs, distribute supplies, and support local relief efforts. Their training in both military operations and humanitarian principles enabled them to navigate the challenging terrain and work effectively with local partners. The mission demonstrated the value of combining military logistics with humanitarian expertise to deliver timely and effective assistance.

Another example is the UK's involvement in the humanitarian response to the Syrian refugee crisis. Humanitarian soldiers were deployed to support refugee camps in neighboring countries, providing medical care, constructing shelters, and ensuring the safety and security of vulnerable populations. Their presence helped to stabilize the camps and facilitate the delivery of aid from humanitarian organizations. The mission underscored the importance of cultural sensitivity and the need to build trust with affected communities.

The UK's response to the COVID-19 pandemic also provides valuable insights into the role of humanitarian soldiers. The military was involved in a wide range of activities, from establishing testing centers and field hospitals to delivering personal protective equipment and supporting vaccination efforts. Humanitarian soldiers played a critical role in these operations, leveraging their logistical expertise and commitment to public health. The pandemic response highlighted the importance of flexibility and adaptability in humanitarian-military cooperation.

In the Caribbean, the UK has deployed humanitarian soldiers to assist with disaster response and recovery following hurricanes and other natural disasters. These missions have involved search and rescue operations, medical assistance, and the reconstruction of critical infrastructure. Humanitarian soldiers have worked closely with local authorities and international partners to ensure a coordinated and effective response. Their efforts have contributed to more resilient communities and faster recovery times.

In summary, these case studies from the UK demonstrate the practical impact of humanitarian soldiers in diverse contexts. Their ability to combine military capabilities with humanitarian principles enables them to address complex challenges and support communities in need. By learning from these experiences and sharing best practices, the UK can continue to enhance the effectiveness of its humanitarian-military cooperation.

7

Chapter 7: The Role of Technology

The role of technology in humanitarian military operations cannot be overstated. In recent years, advancements in technology have transformed the way humanitarian soldiers operate, enabling them to respond more effectively to crises and improve the delivery of aid. From cutting-edge communication tools to advanced medical equipment, technology has become an indispensable part of humanitarian military missions.

One of the key areas where technology has made a significant impact is in communication and coordination. Humanitarian soldiers use sophisticated communication systems to stay connected with headquarters, coordinate with humanitarian organizations, and share real-time information. These systems enable them to respond quickly to changing conditions and ensure that aid is delivered efficiently. In disaster zones, where traditional communication infrastructure may be damaged, satellite phones and portable communication devices are essential tools for maintaining connectivity.

Another important technological advancement is the use of unmanned aerial vehicles (UAVs), commonly known as drones. Drones are used for a variety of purposes, including aerial surveillance, mapping, and delivering supplies to remote or inaccessible areas. They provide humanitarian soldiers with valuable data on the extent of damage, the location of affected populations, and the best routes for delivering aid. In the UK, drones have been deployed in disaster response missions, demonstrating their versatility and effectiveness.

Medical technology has also played a crucial role in enhancing the capabilities of humanitarian soldiers. Portable medical devices, such as ultrasound machines, defibrillators, and diagnostic tools, allow soldiers to provide high-quality medical care in the field. Advances in telemedicine enable medical personnel to consult with specialists remotely, ensuring that patients receive the best possible care. In addition, the development of mobile clinics and field hospitals has improved the ability to provide comprehensive healthcare in disaster and conflict zones.

Technology has also improved the logistics and supply chain management of humanitarian military operations. Humanitarian soldiers use advanced tracking systems to monitor the movement of supplies and ensure that aid reaches its intended destination. Automated inventory management systems help to prevent shortages and optimize the distribution of resources. In the UK, the use of technology in logistics has been a key factor in the success of humanitarian missions, allowing for more efficient and transparent operations.

In summary, technology has become an integral part of humanitarian military operations, enhancing the effectiveness and efficiency of aid delivery. Humanitarian soldiers leverage a wide range of technological tools to improve communication, gather data, provide medical care, and manage logistics. As technology continues to evolve, it will undoubtedly play an even greater role in shaping the future of humanitarian military cooperation.

8

Chapter 8: Collaboration with Humanitarian Organizations

The success of humanitarian military operations often depends on effective collaboration with humanitarian organizations. In the UK, partnerships between the military and organizations such as the Red Cross, Médecins Sans Frontières, and various UN agencies have been instrumental in addressing complex humanitarian crises. These collaborations leverage the strengths of both sectors to deliver more comprehensive and coordinated aid.

One of the key benefits of collaboration is the ability to pool resources and expertise. Humanitarian organizations bring a wealth of knowledge and experience in areas such as medical care, shelter, and nutrition, while the military provides logistical support, security, and infrastructure. By working together, they can deliver aid more effectively and reach a larger number of people in need. This synergy is particularly important in large-scale disasters, where the scale of the response requires a coordinated effort.

Collaboration also enhances the credibility and acceptance of humanitarian military operations. Humanitarian organizations often have established relationships with local communities and a reputation for neutrality and impartiality. Their involvement in military-led missions can help to build trust and ensure that aid is delivered in a manner that respects humanitarian principles. In turn, the military's logistical capabilities can support the work of humanitarian organizations, enabling them to operate more efficiently and safely.

In the UK, joint training exercises and simulations are a key component of fostering collaboration between the military and humanitarian organizations. These exercises provide an opportunity for both sectors to practice working together, share best practices, and develop a common understanding of each other's roles and responsibilities. They also help to build personal relationships and trust, which are essential for effective collaboration in the field.

One example of successful collaboration is the UK's response to the Rohingya refugee crisis. The military and humanitarian organizations worked together to provide shelter, medical care, and food to hundreds of thousands of refugees. Humanitarian soldiers supported the construction of refugee camps, provided medical assistance, and helped to coordinate the delivery of aid. The collaboration between the military and humanitarian organizations was critical to the success of the response and highlighted the importance of working together to address complex crises.

In summary, collaboration with humanitarian organizations is a cornerstone of effective humanitarian military operations. By combining resources, expertise, and credibility, the military and humanitarian organizations can deliver more comprehensive and coordinated aid. The UK's experience demonstrates the value of these partnerships and the importance of fostering collaboration through joint training and exercises.

9

Chapter 9: Gender and Diversity in Humanitarian Military Operations

Gender and diversity play a crucial role in the effectiveness and inclusivity of humanitarian military operations. The UK's military has made significant strides in promoting gender equality and embracing diversity within its ranks. This commitment is reflected in the composition of humanitarian soldiers, who come from a wide range of backgrounds and bring diverse perspectives to their work. By fostering an inclusive environment, the military can better address the needs of diverse populations and ensure that aid is delivered equitably.

One of the key benefits of gender and diversity in humanitarian military operations is the ability to engage more effectively with local communities. Female humanitarian soldiers, in particular, can play a vital role in building trust and fostering communication with women and children in affected areas. Their presence can help to address specific needs related to gender-based violence, reproductive health, and child protection. In the UK, efforts to increase the representation of women in the military have led to more inclusive and responsive humanitarian missions.

Diversity within the ranks of humanitarian soldiers also brings a range of skills and perspectives that enhance the overall effectiveness of operations. Soldiers from different cultural backgrounds can provide valuable insights into the social dynamics and cultural norms of the regions in which they operate. This cultural competence is essential for building trust and ensuring that aid is delivered in a manner that respects local customs and traditions. The UK's diverse military force is well-positioned to navigate these complexities and provide more effective and culturally sensitive assistance.

The promotion of gender and diversity within the military also has important implications for leadership and decision-making. Inclusive leadership can lead to more innovative and effective solutions to complex humanitarian challenges. By drawing on the experiences and perspectives of a diverse group of soldiers, the military can develop strategies that are more holistic and responsive to the needs of affected populations. In the UK, initiatives such as the Women, Peace, and Security agenda have been instrumental in promoting gender equality and diversity in military operations.

In summary, gender and diversity are essential components of effective humanitarian military operations. The UK's commitment to promoting inclusivity within its military has enhanced the ability of humanitarian soldiers to engage with diverse populations and address their specific needs. By fostering an inclusive environment and leveraging the strengths of a diverse force, the military can deliver more equitable and effective humanitarian assistance.

10

Chapter 10: The Future of Humanitarian Military Cooperation

The future of humanitarian military cooperation holds both challenges and opportunities. As global crises continue to evolve in complexity and scale, the need for a coordinated and multifaceted response will only grow. Humanitarian soldiers will play a critical role in addressing these challenges, leveraging their unique training and capabilities to provide effective and principled assistance. The UK's experience provides valuable insights into the future of this cooperation and the steps needed to enhance its effectiveness.

One of the key trends shaping the future of humanitarian military cooperation is the increasing use of technology and innovation. Advances in areas such as artificial intelligence, data analytics, and remote sensing have the potential to revolutionize humanitarian operations. Humanitarian soldiers will need to stay at the forefront of these developments, integrating new technologies into their work and ensuring that they are used ethically and responsibly. The UK's commitment to research and development in the defense sector positions it well to lead in this area.

Another important trend is the growing emphasis on resilience and sustainability in humanitarian efforts. The focus is shifting from immediate relief to long-term recovery and development, with an emphasis on building the capacity of local communities to withstand future crises. Humanitarian soldiers will need to work closely with local partners and communities to support these efforts, ensuring that their interventions are sustainable and contribute to long-term stability. The UK's experience in conflict zones and disaster areas provides valuable lessons for developing effective resilience strategies.

The future of humanitarian military cooperation will also be shaped by the need for greater collaboration and coordination between different actors. This includes not only humanitarian organizations and the military but also governments, the private sector, and civil society. Humanitarian soldiers will need to navigate these complex networks, fostering partnerships and leveraging the strengths of different sectors to deliver comprehensive and coordinated aid. The UK's experience in fostering collaboration provides a model for other countries to follow.

Finally, the future of humanitarian military cooperation will be influenced by the evolving nature of global conflicts and disasters. The increasing frequency and intensity of natural disasters, coupled with ongoing political instability and conflict, will require a flexible and adaptive approach. Humanitarian soldiers will need to be prepared to respond to a wide range of scenarios, from natural disasters to complex emergencies. The UK's ongoing commitment to training and capacity-building will be essential in preparing humanitarian soldiers for these challenges.

In summary, the future of humanitarian military cooperation is filled with both challenges and opportunities. By staying at the forefront of technological innovation, promoting resilience and sustainability, fostering collaboration, and preparing for evolving crises, humanitarian soldiers can continue to play a vital role in addressing global challenges. The UK's experience provides valuable insights and a roadmap for enhancing the effectiveness of humanitarian military cooperation.

11

Chapter 11: Lessons Learned and Best Practices

Over the years, the UK has accumulated valuable lessons and best practices from its humanitarian military operations. These insights provide a foundation for continuous improvement and adaptation, ensuring that future missions are more effective and aligned with humanitarian principles. By reflecting on past experiences and learning from both successes and challenges, humanitarian soldiers can enhance their capabilities and contribute to more positive outcomes in crisis situations.

One of the key lessons learned is the importance of thorough preparation and training. Humanitarian missions are complex and often require rapid responses to dynamic situations. Comprehensive training that includes both military and humanitarian components is essential for equipping soldiers with the skills and knowledge needed to navigate these challenges. This includes scenario-based exercises, cultural sensitivity training, and collaboration with humanitarian organizations. The UK's investment in training programs has been a critical factor in the success of its humanitarian military operations.

Another important lesson is the value of community engagement and local partnerships. Effective humanitarian interventions require an understanding of the local context and the active involvement of affected communities.

Humanitarian soldiers must prioritize building relationships with local leaders, organizations, and residents. This approach not only enhances the credibility and acceptance of the mission but also ensures that aid is tailored to the specific needs and preferences of the community. The UK's experience demonstrates the importance of a community-centered approach to humanitarian military operations.

Flexibility and adaptability are also crucial for success in humanitarian missions. The unpredictable nature of crises means that plans often need to be adjusted on the fly. Humanitarian soldiers must be able to think critically, make informed decisions, and adapt to changing circumstances. This requires a culture of continuous learning and the ability to draw on a diverse set of skills and experiences. The UK's emphasis on flexibility and innovation has enabled its humanitarian soldiers to respond effectively to a wide range of scenarios.

The importance of coordination and collaboration cannot be overstated. Humanitarian missions involve multiple actors, including government agencies, international organizations, NGOs, and local communities. Effective coordination ensures that efforts are aligned, resources are used efficiently, and aid reaches those who need it most. The UK's experience highlights the need for clear communication, joint planning, and the establishment of common goals. By fostering a spirit of collaboration, humanitarian soldiers can contribute to more cohesive and effective responses.

In summary, the UK's experience in humanitarian military operations has yielded valuable lessons and best practices. Preparation, community engagement, flexibility, and collaboration are essential components of successful missions. By incorporating these principles into their operations, humanitarian soldiers can enhance their effectiveness and contribute to more positive outcomes in crisis situations.

12

Chapter 12: A Vision for the Future

As the global landscape continues to evolve, the role of humanitarian soldiers will become increasingly important. The challenges of the future—ranging from climate change and natural disasters to complex conflicts and pandemics—will require a coordinated and multifaceted approach. The UK's experience provides a roadmap for how humanitarian military cooperation can adapt and thrive in this changing environment.

Looking ahead, one of the key priorities will be to strengthen the integration of humanitarian principles into military operations. This involves not only training and education but also the development of policies and protocols that prioritize humanitarian objectives. Humanitarian soldiers must remain committed to principles of neutrality, impartiality, and independence, ensuring that their actions are guided by a commitment to alleviating human suffering.

Innovation and technology will continue to play a central role in shaping the future of humanitarian military operations. The UK's investment in research and development will be essential for staying at the forefront of technological advancements. By leveraging new tools and approaches, humanitarian soldiers can enhance their capabilities and improve the delivery of aid. This includes not only cutting-edge technologies but also the adoption of innovative practices and methodologies.

Collaboration and partnerships will be more important than ever. The complexity of global challenges requires a collective effort, involving a diverse range of actors. Humanitarian soldiers must continue to build strong relationships with humanitarian organizations, governments, the private sector, and local communities. By working together, they can develop more comprehensive and effective responses to crises. The UK's experience in fostering collaboration provides valuable insights for building these partnerships.

Finally, the future of humanitarian military cooperation will depend on a commitment to continuous learning and adaptation. The global landscape is constantly changing, and humanitarian soldiers must be prepared to evolve with it. This involves reflecting on past experiences, embracing new ideas, and being open to feedback and improvement. By fostering a culture of learning and growth, the UK can ensure that its humanitarian soldiers remain at the forefront of effective and principled humanitarian interventions.

In summary, the future of humanitarian soldiers lies in their ability to adapt, innovate, and collaborate. The UK's experience provides a vision for how humanitarian military cooperation can continue to evolve and address the challenges of the future. By staying true to humanitarian principles, leveraging technology, building partnerships, and committing to continuous learning, humanitarian soldiers can play a vital role in creating a more just and resilient world.

Humanitarian Soldiers: When Aid Meets Military in the UK

In this insightful book, explore the evolving convergence of humanitarian aid and military operations in the UK. The work sheds light on the innovative strategies that combine the strengths of both sectors to address global crises effectively.

Chapter 1 delves into the fundamental principles and the changing landscape that has led to the integration of humanitarian and military efforts. **Chapter 2** provides a historical context, tracing the evolution of this relationship from the aftermath of World War I to the present day.

Learn about the comprehensive training programs in **Chapter 3**, which prepare military personnel to become humanitarian soldiers, equipped with both combat skills and humanitarian principles. **Chapter 4** showcases real-life deployments, illustrating the practical application of their training in various conflict zones and disaster areas.

Chapter 5 discusses the ethical dilemmas and challenges faced by humanitarian soldiers, emphasizing the need to balance military objectives with humanitarian principles. **Chapter 6** offers case studies from the UK's recent humanitarian missions, highlighting successful collaborations and impactful interventions.

Discover the transformative role of technology in **Chapter** 7, enhancing communication, medical care, and logistics. **Chapter 8** emphasizes the importance of collaboration with humanitarian organizations, showcasing the benefits of pooling resources and expertise.

Chapter 9 explores the critical role of gender and diversity in humanitarian military operations, highlighting how inclusive practices improve engagement with local communities. **Chapter 10** looks ahead to the future of humanitarian military cooperation, focusing on innovation, resilience, and the need for continuous learning.

Chapter 11 shares valuable lessons learned and best practices from the UK's experience, providing a foundation for future humanitarian missions. Finally, **Chapter 12** presents a vision for the future, outlining the steps needed to enhance the effectiveness of humanitarian soldiers in an ever-changing global landscape.

www.ingramcontent.com/pod-product-compliance
Lightning Source LLC
LaVergne TN
LVHW020743090526
838202LV00057BA/6206